WHEN I WAS YOUR AGE

A play by Mary Moore

Illustrated by Tom Knight

Characters

Mike

Dad
(Uncle Jon to Mike)

Dad: Children, don't forget that your cousin Mike is coming today.

Jenny: Is he nice?

Kim: How old is he?

Dad: He's much older than you. He's grown up now.

Poppy: Will he bring us presents?

Dad: Poppy, don't be so greedy.

Ben: Does he like football?

Dad: I don't know. Oh, there's the doorbell. That must be him.

Dad goes to the door.

Mike: Hi, Uncle Jon!

Dad: Hello, Mike! Come in! Would you like a cup of tea?

Mike: Yes, please.

Dad: I'll go and make it, then, while you say hello to your cousins. Meet Kim, Jenny, Poppy and Ben.

Mike: Hi there. Wow! Are you all … twins? What do they call it if there are four of you?

Jenny: Quadruplets – or quads for short.

Ben: Do you like football, Mike? I love it. I scored three goals yesterday.

Mike: That's nothing. When I was your age I once scored **ten** goals.

Ben: Oh.

Mike: What are the rest of you good at?

Jenny: I like jigsaws. I did one with 300 pieces last week.

Mike: Is that all? When I was your age I could do jigsaws with **1000** pieces.

Jenny: Oh, could you?

Kim: I'm good at maths. I know all my times tables up to ten.

Mike: Well, when I was your age I knew my tables up to **100**.

Poppy: I'm good at swimming. I can swim 100 metres.

Mike: When I was your age, I could swim a **mile**.

Poppy: That's a long way.

Dad enters.

Dad: Here's your cup of tea, Mike – and some chocolate biscuits. Don't eat too many, Ben!

Ben: Okay, Dad. *(turns to Mike)* I love chocolate biscuits. I ate a whole packet yesterday.

Mike: When I was your age, I once ate **five** packets of chocolate biscuits!

Kim: I'm good at cooking. I can cook pancakes all by myself!

Mike: That's nothing. When I was your age, I cooked a **feast** for the **whole** family.

Dad: Really?

Poppy: I like climbing trees. I climbed one three metres high the other day.

Mike: Well, when I was your age, I could climb trees **five** metres high.

Jenny: I like playing computer games.

Kim: Jenny's really good at Crocodile Crunch.

Jenny: Yes, I got up to level seven yesterday.

Mike: When I was your age I got to level **nine** on Crocodile Crunch.

Poppy: (*whispers to Jenny*) But it's only just come out!

Mike: Anyway, how old are you?
Ben: Seven.
Mike: That's nothing. When I was your age, I was **ten**!